Fire-Bellied Toad Care

Photo Credits

Marian Bacon: 4
R. D. Bartlett: 10, 15, 23, 43, 49, 57
Suzanne L. Collins: 1, 19, 28
Paul Donovan: 38
Paul Freed: 30
U. R. Friese: 22
James E. Gerholdt: 17, 20
Barry Mansell: 9
Gerold and Walter Merker: 16
Aaron Norman: 7, 12, 33
Marc Staniszewski: 11, 24
Karl H. Switak: 3, 5, 13, 14, 36, 47, 58 (top), 59
Angela M. Thomas: 51, 53, 58, 61, 62

T.F.H. Publications, Inc.
One TFH Plaza
Third and Union Avenues
Neptune City, NJ 07753

Library of Congress Cataloging-in-Publication Data
Mazorlig, Tom.
Quick & easy fire-bellied toad care / Tom Mazorlig.
p. cm.
Includes index.
ISBN 0-7938-1016-7 (alk. paper)
1. Oriental fire-bellied toads as pets. 2. Bombina as pets. I. Title: Quick and easy fire-bellied toad care. II. Title.
SF459.T54M39 2005
639.3'786--dc22
2004023667

www.tfhpublications.com

Table of Contents

Fire-Bellied Basics

Congratulations on your decision to bring a fire-bellied toad (or a few) into your home. These are charming and easily cared for amphibians who will provide you with hours of fun as you watch their interesting behavior.

Hopefully you bought this book before you actually bought your toads, but even if you didn't, fire-bellies are hardy toads who will be able live in less than ideal conditions for a day or so while you read this book and set them up a nice home. If you already have a fire-belly or three, you should probably skip to the housing and feeding chapters so you can make your toads a proper environment as soon as possible. Be sure to read the rest of the book later,

Herps is the Word

Throughout this book, you will see the term *herps*. This word refers both to reptiles and amphibians and comes from the word *herpetology*, which is the study of these two groups of animals . When speaking of the hobby of keeping reptiles and amphibians, you can call it the *herp hobby*. *Herpetoculture* is the keeping and breeding of reptiles and amphibians. A *herper* is some one who participates in the herp hobby or herpetoculture.

These terms are handy to know, not just for reading this book, but because you will see them in other herp publications and the Internet and hear other hobbyists use them as well.

as it will provide you with a lot of interesting and useful information about your colorful critters.

What's a Fire-bellied Toad?

While you may know what a fire-bellied toad looks like and have perhaps picked out some nice ones from the pet store, you may not know much about them or their habits.

The term *fire-bellied toad* is used for a few species of small, mostly aquatic frogs who have warty skin and brightly colored bellies. Scientists place these frogs in a group called *Bombina*. There are six species in this group, each with its own name and appearance. They are found from the Balkan Mountains in Europe to China, Korea, and Thailand.

The fire-bellied toad most often found in pet stores is the Oriental fire-bellied toad, *Bombina orientalis*. These are pretty little toads with green—sometimes brown—backs with some black markings, and bright red or orange bellies with black blotches. They have

A Frog or a Toad?

If you are ever asked whether your fire-bellies are frogs or toads, you can truthfully answer that they are both. Scientifically, there is no strict difference between frogs and toads, although the term *toad* usually refers to those frogs who have been classified in a few families (mainly Bufonidae, Pelobatidae, and Discoglossidae) that consist mainly of warty, terrestrial frogs. So, all toads are frogs, but not all frogs are toads.

warty skin and prominent eyes. Since these are by far the most common fire-bellied toads in the pet trade, whenever I use *fire-belly* or *fire-bellied toad*, that will be the species I'm talking about. If I want to talk about the other species, I'll use their full names, so you'll know exactly which toad I mean.

The typical fire-bellied toad is bright green with black markings. Some are brown or bronze, and the bronze ones tend to have few black markings.

Scientific Names

You may have noticed that sometimes there are strange-looking words in italics that appear after the name of an animal. This is the scientific name, and each animal only has one scientific name. Biologists determine the scientific name of each animal based on what other animals it is related to. To give a familiar example, dogs are known to scientists as *Canis familiaris*, while their close relatives, wolves, are called *Canis lupis*. The first part of the name is called the *genus*. The second part is the *species*, and this combination of genus and species is unique for each animal.

The reason we have scientific names is so that scientists all over the world can talk about each animal without worrying about language barriers or other similar animals being confused with the one they want to discuss (there are many green tree frogs, but only the small greenish tree frog of eastern North America is called *Hyla cinerea*).

If you use the genus name once, you can abbreviate it to the first letter when you write about it later. So, if I were talking about green tree frogs again, I could just type *H. cinerea*. Also, if I wanted to talk about all the tree frogs in the same genus as the green tree frog, I would just say *Hyla*.

Scientific names are confusing and hard to pronounce at first, but they actually do make things easier. If you decide to do more reading about keeping pet reptiles and amphibians, you should become accustomed to scientific names, since hobbyists use them frequently.

In the United States hobby, two other *Bombina* are sometimes available. The common or European fire-bellied toad, *B. bombina*, has a brown back, pale red-orange belly, and brown toes. The other one that you might see for sale is the yellow-bellied toad, *B. variegata*. This frog has a brown back, a black and yellow belly, and yellow toes.

Family Matters

Until recently, the genus *Bombina*, which contained our friends, the fire-bellied toads, was part of the family Discoglossidae, a family of primitive frogs who cannot flick out their tongues. Research has led scientists to move them to another family called Bombinatoridae. They share this family with one other genus, *Barbourula*. You should be aware of this, so that if you do more reading about fire-bellies, you won't be confused by older works referring them to Discoglossidae.

There are at least six fire-bellied toad species in the world. I say "at least" because new animals are discovered every year, and you never know what could be found out in nature. Also, sometimes after doing some research, biologists discover that one species is actually two very similar species. In the European hobby, the European fire-bellied toad and the giant fire-bellied toad are available, so it is possible that they will someday be more common in the US.

Fire-bellies are alert and active frogs, ready to nab a passing insect or dive into water to escape danger.

As their name suggests, yellow-bellied toads have a more yellowish belly than oriental fire-bellies.

Fire-bellied Life

Oriental fire-bellied toads live in areas of China, Korea, and Russia. They live in and near permanent shallow bodies of water and can be found in fairly mountainous areas, so the water they live in may be quite cool. They are active during the day and will bask in patches of sunlight both on land and when floating on the surface of the water, where they spend much of their time. Captive fire-bellied

Species List

European Fire-bellied Toad	*Bombina bombina*
Guangxi Fire-bellied Toad	*Bombina fortinuptialis*
Giant Fire-bellied Toad	*Bombina maxima*
Hubei Fire-bellied Toad	*Bombina microdeladigitoria*
Oriental Fire-bellied Toad	*Bombina orientalis*
Yellow-bellied Fire-bellied Toad	*Bombina variegata*

toads can live for well over ten years, while those in the wild probably do not live as long due to predation, parasites, disease, and harsh weather conditions.

Fire-bellies are voracious little predators. They will eat just about anything that is moving and small enough to be subdued and consumed—insects, spiders, worms, freshwater shrimp and other crustaceans, smaller frogs and tadpoles, and even tiny fish.

These toads become inactive during the cold winter months, but they don't truly hibernate. When the weather warms, they mate and lay eggs. The eggs hatch into tadpoles; the tadpoles are scavengers, eating whatever they can find. In a few weeks, the tadpoles grow legs, leave the water, and continue to eat and grow until they mate and continue the cycle.

European fire-bellied toads are brown with an orange belly. They are more common in the European and Asian reptile trades than in the US.

The most distinctive fire-belly is undoubtedly the giant fire-bellied toad. None of the other species grow so large or have such huge tubercles.

Toxic Toads

The bright colors of the fire-bellied toads did not evolve to make them more appealing to human pet keepers. They evolved as a way to avoid being eaten by other animals. You see, fire-bellied toads (and almost all frogs, to one extent or another) produce toxic chemicals in their skin. These chemicals are at least irritating and sometimes even lethal to predators who consume a toad. The bright colors serve as a warning that the fire-bellies are dangerous to eat.

When a fire-bellied is threatened, he will perform a strange behavior that shows the predator his bright belly, hopefully convincing the predator he is too dangerous to eat. This behavior is called the *unken-reflex*. The toad arches his back and pulls his legs up so that his brilliant orange underside is visible. This display reveals his toxic nature to his foes and may prevent his demise. If the predator does go on to eat the poor fire-belly, he is likely to become very ill, and probably won't mess with fire-bellies again.

Does this mean that fire-bellies are dangerous pets? Not really. To be affected by the toad's venom, you must ingest it or get it into some other orifice. Since you are not likely to eat your toads, you should have little to worry about. However, some people are sensitive to the chemicals amphibians produce, and contact with them may cause a rash or irritation. These people should use gloves when handling the toads or performing tank maintenance.

Similarly, if you have an open wound on your hand and you come in contact with the toads or their tank water, the wound is likely to burn, sting, and/or tingle. Again, the use of gloves will prevent this. Always wash your hands after handling the toads or maintaining the tank; rubbing your eyes when there are toad toxins on your hands is no fun.

Fire-bellies as Pets

Fire-bellied toads make wonderful pet amphibians. They are undemanding, quiet, odorless (provided you perform regular cleaning of the enclosure), inexpensive, and long-lived. They are also among the hardiest amphibians. Unless neglected or housed inappropriately,

The yellow-bellied toad is found over much of central and eastern Europe. This individual was found in Italy.

they will thrive. Fire-bellies are active and diurnal, so you will have hours of entertainment watching them hop about, hunt, swim, squabble, and mate.

While they are not social in the same sense that mammals and birds are social, fire-bellies do well in small groups. If you are buying a fire-bellied toad, consider getting a small group. They won't take up much more room than one would and will allow you to see more natural behaviors as you more closely mimic the wild situation these frogs would be in.

Fire-bellies are bold little critters. Over time, they will become accustomed to your presence and will stop trying to hop away from your hand when you feed them or perform maintenance on the terrarium. Some may become tame enough to eat out of your hand.

However, fire-bellies and most amphibians are not pets in the same way cats or dogs are. They are too small to really be handled, and their skin secretions may irritate your skin. They are best thought of as interesting animals to watch and care for.

The bright bellies of fire-bellied toads warn predators that they are toxic.

When fire-bellies are threatened, they expose their warning colors by lifting up their feet and curving their back—usually more dramatically than in this photo.

The vast majority of fire-bellied toads in the hobby are captured in the wild and exported to the US from China. Although some hobbyists breed them, fire-bellies are not yet produced on a commercial scale, as are some other frogs, like the Argentine horned frog. It is best to buy herps who have been produced in captivity. These are called captive-bred individuals, and they are more desirable because they have not been in the wild, and therefore there is a much smaller risk they carry parasites and diseases. Additionally, if you buy captive-bred herps, you are not taking animals from the wild, which may put stress on their populations and lead to their decline. Unfortunately, it is difficult to find captive-bred fire-bellied toads, so keepers usually settle for wild-caught ones. Fire-bellied toads are still abundant in the wild, so for now, the trade in wild ones doesn't seem to be harming them.

Selecting a Fire-bellied Toad

Fire-bellied toads are most often purchased at pet stores, although you may also see them at herp shows. The rules for picking out healthy ones are practically the same in either situation.

This is a plump and healthy-looking fire-bellied toad who will be likely to thrive with proper captive care.

You should first evaluate the knowledge and conscientiousness of the vendor. After reading this book, you'll know how to keep fire-bellies healthy and happy. Look to see whether the vendor is providing a proper environment for his or her fire-bellies. If the conditions are wrong or the cage is dirty, take your business elsewhere. Similarly, if there are dead animals in the cage (especially if they are not freshly dead), you really don't want to give that vendor your business. If the store smells bad or has other animals that are housed incorrectly or are obviously ill or undernourished, that proprietor does not deserve your money. Inquire whether the animals in the store are guaranteed, and if so, for how long. Most pet stores will replace animals who are sick or who die within the first few days or possibly week after the animal leaves the store. If the store doesn't guarantee their animals, this might be a sign of a poor store to purchase your toads from.

Once you have determined that the store or show vendor is taking proper care of the toads and other animals, you will want to pick out healthy fire-bellies. Like most herps, fire-bellies hide signs of illness very well. It is possible to pick out one who seems to be the picture of health only to have him succumb to some illness in a week or two. However, by selecting only the healthiest-appearing individuals, you significantly reduce the chance of having a problem.

Watch the toads who are on display. Take note of which ones are active and appear alert. Ask if the employee will feed them, and then watch which ones eat. Fire-bellies are enthusiastic eaters, so avoid any individual who doesn't at least chase after prey.

Healthy fire-bellies are not skinny. You shouldn't be able to see the hipbones or the spine. The eyes should be clear and not cloudy, closed, or inflamed. Look at the toes for signs of injury and infection. Because fire-bellies are taken from the wild, they may be missing toes due to run-ins with predators or damage in capture; as long as the toe stump has healed, a missing toe is no cause for alarm.

It is best for your toad if you have his home all set up before you buy him and bring him home.

Once you have found a toad or several that seem healthy, show the vendor which ones you want, make sure he catches the right ones, pay for them, and take them home.

Coming Home

It is better by far to have the captive environment set up before buying the toads. This allows you to ensure your environmental parameters are correct before subjecting a living creature to them. It also means your toads will spend less time in a less-than-ideal transport container than if you have to set up the enclosure after bringing the toads home.

Most of the time, fire-bellied toads are sold in a plastic bag with a little water and some air in it. It is best if they are sold to you in ventilated deli cups with moist paper towels in the bottom. In either case, get the fire-bellies home as soon as possible after purchase, and avoid temperature extremes during transit. Fire-bellies are more tolerant of cold than of heat, so if it is hot out, you might consider sending someone ahead to the car to turn on the air conditioner. If you are buying them in the winter, you can put the container of toads inside your jacket until you get home.

Once you get them home, place the container into the terrarium, open it carefully—fire-bellies jump—and gently scoop the toads out into their new home. If the toads soiled themselves during the journey, you may want to scoop them out into a container of dechlorinated water (see the housing sections for details) before placing them into the terrarium.

Housing Your Fire-Bellied Toads

Most animals have adapted to live in a specific natural habitat that is, more than likely, nothing like the interior of your house. When bringing any pet reptile or amphibian into your home, you are obligated to provide the animal with a captive environment in which he can thrive. To do anything else is inhumane.

Fortunately, fire-bellied toads are adaptable little creatures, and their housing requirements are not too strict. As we have discussed, they have adapted to live in shallow ponds and streams in temperate to subtropical regions. Their basic environmental requirements are a land area, a swimming area, and a proper

No Sunlight

When placing your fire-bellied toad enclosure, put it in an area that does not get direct sunlight. Sunlight shining in the tank can lead to a sudden rise in temperature, since the glass or plastic will retain the heat. This can stress out or even kill your toads.

temperature. Yes, there is more to it than this short list, but those are the bare bones of what fire-bellies need. None of these requirements are difficult to provide.

Two Methods

Because fire-bellies are adaptable and hardy, there are quite a few ways to house them successfully. These can be broken into two general types—simplistic and elaborate—and both have their pluses and minuses.

Simplistic

The simplistic method of housing has the advantage of being, well, simple. This is a bare bones type setup, with no attempt to recreate the habitat of fire-bellies. This type of setup is most often used in pet stores and herp wholesale facilities, as it is easy to maintain and prevents escapees.

Sphagnum moss makes a good substrate for fire-bellied toads whether your terrarium is simple or elaborate.

Generally, the simplistic setup consists of the cage itself, a moisture-retaining substrate, and some form of temperature control Usually the substrate is wet paper towels or sphagnum moss. These substrates are cheap and easy to clean: Simply take out the substrate, discard it, rinse out the enclosure, add new substrate, and moisten. Nothing could be easier.

The disadvantages to this are that the toads have little opportunity to perform natural behaviors, such as swimming, diving, hiding, and breeding. Additionally, this setup is hardly attractive to the human viewer. The last disadvantage is that the cage will need to be cleaned frequently. If you use paper towels as the substrate, you will need to clean the cage daily or every other day, depending on the number of toads. If you use the moss, you will probably be able to go an extra day or two between cleanings.

Elaborate

The elaborate enclosure attempts to provide the fire-bellied toads with a more complex and naturalistic dwelling. It provides the toads with more opportunities to perform natural behaviors, is much more interesting and pleasurable to human viewers, and doesn't have to be cleaned as frequently. The elaborate setup can also be called a naturalistic one.

It is also more expensive and time-consuming to set up the terrarium and more labor intensive to clean; however, you will be cleaning less often. And because you are dealing with a more complicated system, more things can go wrong: one type of plant could take over, the water could have an algae bloom, the frogs may kick too much substrate in the water and foul it, etc.

It must also be noted that though the elaborate setup is considered naturalistic, it is impossible to provide a truly natural environment to captive fire-bellies. You simply do not have the space or access to all the proper species of plants found with fire-bellies. What you are creating is a complex habitat that mimics enough features of the natural habitat of the toads that they will feel at home enough to act as they would in the wild.

The Enclosure

You can choose from a number of enclosures for your fire-bellies. Most keepers house their toads in a glass aquarium; these are readily available and affordable, but they are fragile and heavy. Still, they are usually the best bet for fire-bellies. Plastic or acrylic cages, like the ones sold at most pet stores, are adequate but hardly ideal. They are small and lack any easy way to light or heat them.

Land and Water

Fire-bellied toads spend a lot of their time in the water, so the most natural setup for them would be a half land and half water terrarium (also called an aquaterrarium). If you are using the simplistic setup, the substrate will be moist enough for the toads, and you needn't worry about having a large water area.

The easiest way to provide your toads with a suitable water area is to give them a large water bowl. Change it daily, as the toads will foul it quickly, and arrange a way for the toads to enter and leave it safely. The simplest method is to have some stones or driftwood breaking the surface of the water, so the toads can climb up and out.

When given sufficient space and enough food, fire-bellies do well in small groups. This makes for a more interesting display.

All species of fire-bellies spend much of their time in the water. A European fire-belly is pictured here.

The most naturalistic and visually interesting way to provide for your toads' semi-aquatic lifestyle is to use a divider to make a land and water section of the cage. You can do this by purchasing a piece of acrylic or glass and cementing it into place about midway across the tank. Most pet stores sell silicon gel to seal aquarium leaks; this is a safe adhesive for fixing the divider in place. You can either slant it like a natural shoreline or arrange it vertically. If you choose the vertical method, your cage furnishings must be placed so that the toads can enter and exit the water when they wish.

How Many?

If you are using a glass aquarium, about five fire-bellies can live comfortably in a standard 10-gallon tank. You can adjust the number for the size tank you have.

Remember that horizontal space is more important than vertical space. A 20-gallon "high" tank can hold no more fire-bellies than a 10-gallon, but a 20-gallon long can hold about eight because of the greatly increased floor space.

Because of the increasing popularity of herps as pets, some companies actually manufacture tanks that have dividers built in for semi-aquatic setups. These are not common yet, but your pet store should be able to order one for you.

A fire-bellied toad's water area should be two to six inches deep. Do not use water fresh out of the tap for your toads. The chlorine is not good for them. To eliminate the chlorine, you can either let the water sit out overnight, allowing the chlorine to disperse into the air, or you can add some of the water dechlorinators sold for use with tropical fish. Another way to avoid chlorine is to just use bottled spring water for your toads, but this may be too expensive an option.

Filtration

The use of a filter in an aquaterrarium is highly recommended. This will save you from having to clean the water so frequently and will make your toads' environment cleaner. Filters also help oxygenate the water. Any one of a number of different types of filters can be used for fire-bellied toads. Fully submersible ones are probably the best to use, as the low water level in a fire-belly tank makes using other types problematic. When buying or using a filter, make sure

Include plants or driftwood in the water section so that your fire-bellies can exit the water easily.

Water is Heavy!

If you are setting your toads up in a naturalistic aquaterrarium, remember that all that water and substrate will be very heavy. You will need a sturdy aquarium stand or other similar piece of furniture.

Put the tank in its location before adding the water and substrate; otherwise, it will be too heavy and fragile to move. And you don't want to drop a tank full of water and gravel on your carpeting!

that there can be no danger of the filter sucking up one of the toads and that any tubes or wires leading in and out of the tank cannot provide a means for the toads to escape. Fire-bellies can push themselves through very small openings, so be careful.

When using a filter, remember that they were designed for fish and not frogs. Frogs produce much more waste than fish. The filter and the water will need to be changed more frequently for fire-bellies than the directions on the filter will state.

Substrates

Which substrate (ground covering of the tank) you use for your fire-bellies depends on the type of setup you are using for them. If you are keeping them in a simplistic enclosure, you will be using paper towels or sphagnum moss.

For an aquaterrarium, you can use aquarium gravel for the aquatic section. Dark colors will show off the colors of the fire-bellied toads the best. Use a small grade gravel rather than one composed of larger particles or pebbles. You can also leave the tank bottom of the water section bare, which makes water changes easier. For the land section, you can also use the gravel, but cover it with a thick layer of sphagnum moss.

No Distilled Water!

Never use distilled water for your toads. Distilled water is water that has had all dissolved particles removed from it via steam distillation. While this may sound like the purest water and therefore good for your toads, it is actually too pure. There are no dissolved minerals in it, and this will create great imbalances and possibly kill your toads. Use dechlorinated tap water or bottled spring water (not purified water) instead.

If you want a very natural-looking enclosure, you can use soil for the land area. Put an inch or two of aquarium gravel on the bottom of the land section, and cover this with the soil to a depth of two inches or more. Then cover that with a deep layer of sphagnum moss. This type of substrate is beneficial for any live plants you might want to use.

Do not use just any soil. Use a sterile, organic potting soil, and make sure it contains no Styrofoam or perlite; both of these substances can harm your toads if ingested. You can find this type of soil at well-stocked gardening stores or some natural groceries.

Temperature and Humidity

No matter what setup you choose for your toads, you have to provide the right environmental conditions for them. The most important of these conditions are temperature and humidity. With fire-bellies, these conditions are not difficult to maintain.

Fire-bellies will be fine at normal room temperatures, though they would prefer temperatures just slightly warmer. An ideal temperature would be 75°F at the warmest spot of the tank. This can be established by putting a low-wattage lamp at one end of the tank, which will make that end warmer and allow the frogs to move back and forth along a temperature gradient as they feel the need.

Place the lamp over the land section, not the water section; the water should be substantially cooler than the rest of the tank. Use a good thermometer, don't guess. People usually underestimate how warm things are, so if it feels fine to you, the temperature actually might be cooking your fire-bellies.

At night, shut off any lights used to heat the terrarium. The toads do best when given a nighttime drop in temperatures. As long as your house temperatures do not drop below 60°F at night, the toads will not need any heat. Shutting off the light at night also maintains the toads' normal circadian rhythms.

If you are keeping your fire-bellies in an aquaterrarium, the humidity will more or less take care of itself. If the toads start to feel too dry, they can simply enter the water. If you are using a large bowl or other container for the water area, use a plant sprayer to mist the tank at least once a day, and don't allow the substrate to dry out.

Decorations

The decorations you choose for you fire-bellied toad cage are limited only by your taste and your toads' safety. Any of the various decorations for sale at your local pet store should be suitable.

Although fire-bellied toads are outgoing little creatures, they enjoy having some hiding places. You can buy nice looking artificial caves, halved coconut shells, or artificial plants to provide them with some hiding areas. Sections of cork bark also make natural-looking hiding areas and are usually not expensive.

Driftwood gives a nice touch to a naturalistic setup. You can use it as a bridge between the land and the water, or just to provide your frogs with some climbing areas. Wood collected from outside is generally not suitable, as it tends to rot in the high humidity inside a fire-belly toad tank.

There are some nice high-quality artificial plants on the market that make good terrarium decorations. They are easier to keep and clean than real plants, and the toads may not notice the difference.

Live plants

To make a truly naturalistic habitat for your toads, consider adding some live plants. A few plants can really bring your terrarium to life. Given your toads' semi-aquatic lifestyle, you can use both terrestrial and aquatic plants.

If you include plants in your setup, you must give them proper lighting. Plants will need at least one fluorescent plant bulb to provide them with enough light to thrive; some plants will require more.

Terrestrial Plants

Several types of houseplants are suitable for fire-bellied toad tanks. However, most houseplants have been treated with an array of pesticides, fertilizers, and other nasty chemicals that might harm your toads. To avoid exposing your toads to these hazards, wash the plant off before placing it in the terrarium. Remove the plant from the pot, rinse all the dirt off the roots, wash the leaves with mild soapy water, and rinse thoroughly (note

Driftwood is an attractive decoration for a fire-belly toad terrarium; it helps to create a natural look.

that sometimes plants die after this procedure, but most usually bounce back). If you are going to put the plant in a pot in the terrarium, repot the plant in a clean pot with the organic potted soil recommended previously. Bury the pot in the substrate to hide it.

While they are terrestrial frogs, fire-bellied toads (giant fire-belly is pictured) will occasionally climb when given the opportunity.

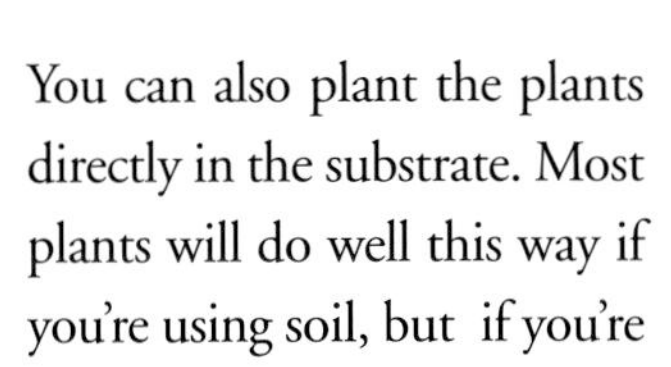

You can also plant the plants directly in the substrate. Most plants will do well this way if you're using soil, but if you're using just moss and gravel, there are still a few types of plants that will thrive, notably pothos, lucky bamboo, and elephant ears. Numerous books and websites about houseplants and even using plants in terraria exist. Consult some of these for more information, if desired.

Aquatic Plants

Some nice aquatic plants will enhance the appearance of the water section of the terrarium. If you are hoping to breed your fire-bellies, aquatic plants will help ensure success, and a nice selection of aquatic plants are available at pet stores with good fish departments. Many aquatic plants come with metal sinkers to help hold them down. These should be removed and the bottom of the plant's stem covered with gravel to keep it in place. If there are any dead leaves or crushed portions of the stem, remove them before putting them in the tank. For more details on growing aquatic plants, there are numerous books and websites available; fish-focused pet stores also have good information. Some recommended aquatic plants are bacopa or water hyssop, anacharis (just allow this plant to float in the water), *Gymnocoronis spilanthoides*, banana plant, and java fern (a plant tolerant of low light conditions). Any little snails or invertebrates hitchhiking on the plants likely will become snacks for your toads.

Maintenance

The maintenance of your toad tank depends largely on how you have it set up. The simplistic type of enclosure is the easiest; just replace the substrate every other day or so, rinse out the enclosure, and add fresh moistened substrate.

Drain or siphon the water out of the aquatic section whenever it gets dirty. If you are using a filter, this will probably be about once a week or ten days. If you do not have a filter, you will have to change the water every three or four days. Remember that frogs produce a lot of waste. When changing the water, stir up the gravel and try to siphon out as much of the muck as possible.

In the naturalistic aqua-terrarium, change the water in the aquatic section with about the same frequency as you would for an all-water setup.

Anacharis will grow nicely when allowed to float on the surface of the water.

The land section will need less maintenance. Remove frog droppings as soon as you see them, replace any sphagnum moss when it becomes unsightly or smelly, and wipe down the tank glass as needed.

About once every six months, you will have to break down the tank completely. First, remove the inhabitants to a suitable holding cage. Throw out all the soil and replace it with new. Rinse all the gravel thoroughly, until it doesn't make the water cloudy, and disinfect all the

Tank Mates

The following is a list of some species that should do well in a fire-bellied toad environment, though there may be others that will work also. Research each species' requirements before you decide to add it to your fire-bellies' habitat.

Fish

Paradise fish	*Macropodus opercularus*
Pleco	*Hypostomus plecostomus*

Frogs

Green tree frog	*Hyla cinerea*
African dwarf clawed frog	*Hymenochirus boetgeri*

Newts

Fire-bellied newt	*Cynops pyrrhogaster*
Eastern newt	*Notophthalmus viridescens*

Lizards**

Green anole*	*Anolis carolinensis*

* This species requires some heat. They will not be comfortable at room temperature.

** Most lizards require ultraviolet light

furnishings and decorations by soaking them in a 10 percent solution of bleach. Rinse them until there are no traces of bleach.

Multispecies Setup

Some keepers like to mix different species of animals together; they say it gives the appearance of a more natural setting. However, this can be dangerous for the creatures, as not all animals get along. Also, when dealing with fire-bellies, remember that they do produce toxins. Still, having several species cohabitating makes for a beautiful and fascinating terrarium.

If you decide to mix in some other animals, there are a few guidelines to follow. First, all of the animals have to have similar care

Care Schedule

Daily

- Turn on lights in morning, off at night
- Check toads for health
- Feed (can be done every other day)
- Remove any droppings

Every Other Day

- Replace paper towels (simplistic setup)

Weekly

- Change water
- Trim any live plants if needed
- Check condition of sphagnum moss and replace if needed

requirements. Second, all should be of similar size to prevent them from eating each other or out-competing each other for food. Third, the keeper must be prepared to give the different species their own cages should the mixing not work out. Lastly, remember that mixing different species is by its nature experimental and that some experiments do fail.

To properly accommodate the different inhabitants, you must use a large enclosure. Consider a 30-gallon aquarium the minimum size for a mixed-species terrarium, especially if you are including fish. The following is a list of some species that should do well in a fire-bellied toad environment, though there may be others that will work also. Research each species' requirements before you decide to add it to your fire-bellies' habitat.

Feeding Your Fire-Bellied Toads

Like all other frogs and toads, fire-bellies eat other animals. Because of their small size, they are limited to eating small prey. In the wild, this would include insects and insect larvae, spiders, earthworms, small crustaceans, and tiny fish—any animal that is small enough for them to stuff in their mouths.

Fire-bellied toads obtain their bright colors from the pigments in the small crustaceans they eat. If you want your fire-bellies to retain their brilliant colors, you will have to feed them foods that contain some of these pigments. This is not too difficult, and we'll discuss how it's done in more detail later in this chapter.

In captivity, the keeper has to provide his or her toads with their prey. Most pet stores carry crickets and mealworms. Many pet stores also carry wax worms, and some sell earthworms. You can add more variety to your toads' diet by purchasing some live fish foods and collecting insects and other small invertebrates from outdoors. Some live fish foods that pet stores may carry include brine shrimp, black worms, bloodworms, and tubifex worms.

Crickets are probably the easiest things to feed your fire-bellies. You can find them at almost any pet store, and they are relatively inexpensive. Crickets are sold in a number of sizes; get ones small enough for your fire-bellies to eat without difficulty. For adult fire-bellies, this usually means those labeled as one-halves or three-quarters, names that describe how close the crickets are to full-grown. Most fire-bellies can consume fully-grown crickets, but it is quite the battle for them to subdue and ingest this size of prey. It is best for your toads to eat smaller, more easily managed food.

Gut-loading and Cricket Care

While crickets make a good staple diet, there are some problems with them. Many pet stores do not keep their crickets in the best of conditions, so by the time you get them home, the crickets may not have had anything—except maybe a piece of apple or potato—to eat for several days. They are, nutritionally, little more than bags of protein and water, lacking fats and many vitamins and minerals. Fed on these nutrient-deficient insects, your fire-bellies are sure to suffer nutritional problems eventually. Additionally, fire-bellied toads (and

Food Size

As a rule of thumb, do not feed your fire-bellied toads any prey items that are larger than their heads. Anything larger may result in regurgitation and possible injury to your toads.

most other predators) depend on the nutritious semi-digested food in the digestive tract of their prey for another significant fraction of their vitamins and minerals. Crickets eat a lot and digest quickly; the starved crickets from many pet stores have essentially no gut contents to speak of.

Tropical fish flakes can be used as one component of the diet for your feeder crickets.

To give your fire-bellied toads a more complete diet, you will have to feed nutritious foods to the crickets prior to feeding them to your toads. It may seem strange to have to feed the food items; welcome to the hobby of keeping insectivorous animals. Because you are packing the digestive tracts of the prey items with nutritious foods, the process of feeding the crickets a good-quality diet is called gut-loading.

Crickets eat practically anything, and that makes them very easy to gut-load. You simply need to give them a few nutritious foodstuffs and allow them to feed on the items for a day or so. Vary what you feed your crickets with each batch to ensure that your toads are getting a well-rounded diet. Grains, such as wheat germ and oatmeal, are a good staple for gut-loading, as are powdered instant baby cereals. You can also use the alfalfa pellets sold as food for rabbits; these work best if you crush or grind them first.

To this base add a nutritious vegetable or two. Greens, such as kale, collard greens, mustard greens, and dandelions, are among the most nutritious foods you can give the crickets. Since fire-bellied toads get their coloration from the carotenes in their food, feeding the crickets bright red and orange fruits and vegetables will help the toads maintain their beautiful colors. Some suggested colorful fruits and vegetable are carrots, oranges, sweet potatoes, red and orange bell peppers, and beets. You do not need chop up the vegetables first; the crickets will nibble at them as they are. The exception is fruits with a hard skin, like oranges. These are best cut into sections. Since fruits and vegetables have such high water contents, there is no need to give the crickets another source of water, provided you keep the vegetables fresh.

At this point, you have probably realized that in order to properly gut-load the feeder crickets, you will need to keep them for a day or two. Like many other herp keepers, you will probably find it easiest to buy more crickets than you need for one feeding, set them up in their own cage, and feed them out as your toads need them. Crickets are easy to keep and if kept clean and well fed, do not smell or have a high mortality rate.

Crickets can be kept in small quarters, depending on how many you are keeping at one time. For a small group of fire-bellied toads, you shouldn't need a cricket cage that is larger than a 2-

In nature, fire-bellies spend much of their time searching for food in the water and on the shore.

Spicy Food

Some keepers claim that adding paprika to the cricket food every so often keeps their herps in good color.

gallon or 5-gallon aquarium. You will need a screen lid made of fine mesh to prevent the crickets from climbing—or jumping—out. Cover the bottom in a thin layer of the grains, and put the vegetables on a small paper plate or jar lid—something to keep them from sitting in the grains and making them soggy. The crickets will do best with some form of hiding area. You can use the tubes from paper towels and toilet paper or crumpled newspaper. Once you have added the hiding areas, your cricket cage is complete. You now have a supply of food available to feed your toads as needed.

Like all animals, crickets do generate waste. Additionally, a few crickets in each batch will die. Clean the cricket cage weekly. Pick out cricket bodies as soon as you notice them. It is best to clean the cricket cage after feeding out the last cricket. This greatly simplifies the process, as you won't have to worry about escaping crickets.

To clean the cage, dump out the contents into a trashcan. Throw away the hiding areas and start with fresh ones. About once a month, or if there is still old food or cricket bodies stuck to the bottom of the cricket cage, perform a more thorough cleaning and disinfection. To do this, scrape away any stuck-on material (you can use a putty knife or spatula—just don't use it for human food preparations again), then soak the cage bottom in a solution of bleach and water (use about 10 percent bleach). Allow this to soak for at least 15 minutes. Afterwards, rinse thoroughly until there is no more bleach smell in the cage.

Allow the cage to dry before adding more crickets and cricket food. You may find it convenient to have another cricket cage and alternate between the two of them; that way, you always have a clean and dry cage waiting.

Crickets and other insects are fed to fire-bellied toads by simply tossing an appropriate number into the cage. The toads will chase them down and gorge themselves.

Care of Mealworms

Although they are not as nutritious as crickets, mealworms are easy for the toad keeper to deal with. They also breed readily, allowing you to keep a source of food on hand at all times.

Mealworms are not actually worms. They are the larva of a small beetle, the darkling beetle, and are frequent pests of flour, meal, grain, and related products. While some fire-bellies accept the beetles as food, the larval form is more valuable as a food source.

Mealworms are usually sold at pet stores and bait shops in pre-portioned cups (usually 250 or 500). Normally they are refrigerated because the cold prevents the larva from changing into the adult

Fire-bellied toads are enthusiastic feeders and will quickly pursue their prey.

Feeding Frenzy

If you have a group of fire-bellied toads, observe them at feeding time. Fire-bellies eat with great enthusiasm, and in their frenzy sometimes mistake a tankmate's leg for a cricket. Gently break up any such mishaps before one of your toads is injured. Likewise, watch to be sure that each toad gets his fair share of food.

beetles. You can keep your mealworms in the refrigerator, or not, as you choose.

Pet stores and mealworm farms often pack the mealworms in sawdust. When you get your mealworms home, remove them from this material, as it does not serve the mealworms as a food source. Place your worms in a container partially filled with wheat germ, oatmeal, or whole grain flour. It needs to be deep enough for the worms to burrow down into it, about three inches or so. You don't need to cover the container (although most keepers do), since the mealworms can't climb out, and the adult beetles very rarely leave the grains. For moisture and added nutrients, put a few slices of carrot, sweet potato, or squash on top of the grain. Throw out the old slices of vegetable and replace them with new ones about every other day to prevent the formation of mold. If the mealworms consume moldy grain, it might hurt your fire-bellies.

Left undisturbed for a month or two, many of the worms will have transformed into beetles, mated, and laid eggs. You should have a nice mix of sizes of worms, adults, and pupae. Other than changing the vegetables, there is little other maintenance required for your mealworm colony. Periodically, you will need to add more grain as the quantity of food decreases. About once every six months or so, sort through the mixture and pick out as many worms and beetles as you can, throw out the old grain (realizing you will be throwing out some worms and eggs at the same time), and start the colony again with fresh grain.

While the colony is churning along, feed out some worms to your toads. Use mealworms for variety in the diet, not as the staple food, since they are low in some nutrients and too high in hard-to-digest chitin. Because the mealworms are not the staple food, you won't be feeding out enough of them to deplete your colony.

It is best to feed mealworms to your toads in a shallow bowl. If they are just left in the cage, they will burrow into the substrate and hide from your toads. Some will end up in the water, drown, and become a disgusting mess. If your toads are tame, they may eat a mealworm or two right from your hand.

Other Insects

Some pet stores and online reptile supply companies carry other insect prey. If you find these items, consider purchasing them, as they are good to feed your toads for variety. Remember that in nature, fire-bellied toads eat many different species of prey. To help ensure that your toads are getting a complete diet, try to offer as many types of prey as possible.

Wax worms, like mealworms, are really a larval insect—in this case, a moth. They are white grubs that look like fat maggots. They are beehive pests and consume beeswax and larval bees. Because of their specialized diet, they are difficult to gut-load and to raise; thus, they are best bought in small quantities and fed to your toads immediately. Wax worms are high in fat and low in many nutrients, so do not feed them to your toads too often.

Silkworms are the caterpillars of the silk moth. They get large (about as long as a fire-bellied toad, or longer!), so only the young ones make good food for fire-bellies. They also tend to be expensive food, so you will probably want to use them just as a

Softer Food

Because mealworms are high in chitin—the major component of their exoskeleton and a substance that is difficult for your toads to digest—it is best to feed out the soft, white mealworms you will sometimes find in your colony. These worms have just molted and have a lower chitin content than normal.

treat. However, they are one of the most nutritious insects you can feed to herps, largely because they dine only on the vitamin- and mineral-rich leaves of mulberry trees. Commercially raised silkworms are fed a prepared diet that is made mostly of these leaves. Because of their specialized diet, silkworms are another prey species that is best to feed to your toads immediately, though online silkworm suppliers have complete instructions for the rearing of silkworms if this is something you would like more information about.

Feed out wax worms and silkworms the same way you would mealworms: in a shallow bowl, or by hand.

If you want to breed your fire-bellied toads or have acquired some tiny ones that have just left the water, you will probably want to buy some colonies of flightless fruit flies. These tiny insects have been selectively bred to have stunted wings. They cannot fly, but they can make long hops. Fruit flies are easy insects to deal with, as they are usually sold in pre-made colonies. Simply dump some flies into your toads' terrarium and leave the colony alone otherwise. To prevent too many flies from escaping, shake or tap the container before opening the lid; this will knock the flies down to the bottom. Each fruit fly colony is good for a few weeks. To encourage the fruit flies to stay in the toads' terrarium—as opposed to walking up the sides and out into your living room—you can put a small piece of fruit (banana or melon works nicely) in the feeding bowl. Most of the flies stay near this source of food.

Sometimes flightless houseflies (called "bungee bugs") are offered for sale. These can be treated exactly like the fruit flies.

You can collect insects from your yard or other wild space if you are careful. The first thing you must do is be sure that you are collecting from an area that has not been sprayed or treated with any pesticides, fungicides, fertilizers, weed-killers, or other toxins. You don't want to harm your toads by exposing them to nasty chemicals.

Remember to feed only insects that are the proper size for your toads—nothing too big. Be careful of what invertebrates you collect; some could be dangerous for your toads. These would include centipedes, which have a nasty bite, and large spiders. Avoid any insects that are brightly colored; such colors usually advertise toxicity. Do not feed out any caterpillars that are fuzzy or spiky. Some invertebrates that are good for your toads to eat are pill bugs, grubs, inchworms, small snails, and aphids.

Most wild-collected insects can be fed to your toads by letting them loose in the cage for the toads to find. If you collect any worms or grubs, feed them to your toad in a shallow dish to prevent them from escaping. Feeding by hand is also an option.

Other Foods

You can feed a number of other animals to your toads besides insects. Because of the convenience, availability, and low cost, most owners stick with insects, but this does deprive your toads of some variety. At least one or two of the foods mentioned in this section will be available at any pet store that carries tropical fish.

Worms

You may find a number of live worms at your local pet store. They include black worms, white worms, tubifex worms, and bloodworms (which are really an insect larva, but they fit best in this section). These worms are usually sold in portions with some water

Yellow-bellied toads and the other species often catch and eat their prey in the water.

and kept refrigerated. It is best to buy only enough of these worms to feed your toads at once. They require frequent water changes, or they quickly die and become foul. It is easier to just feed them and be done with it.

Bloodworms deserve some special mention. Their name comes from their bright red color. Like the bright vegetables mentioned for gut-loading crickets, bloodworms are high in carotenes. Feeding these worms to your toads will help them retain their bright colors. Bloodworms are especially useful for feeding toadlets to grant them the normal, striking colors of fire-bellied toads. Bloodworms can be purchased frozen in packages, and toadlets will usually be willing to accept thawed specimens if they are picked up on a paintbrush and waved around in front of them.

Hand-feeding

Many fire-bellies will become tame enough to hand-feed. If your toads are this tame, you can hand-feed strips of fish, lean meat, and frozen worms to them.

The worms discussed here should not just be dropped into your toads' cage. They will rapidly burrow into the substrate and your toads will never find them. Eventually they will die and cause your cage to become foul more quickly than it would otherwise. Feed them in a shallow bowl or jar lid with just a tiny amount of water. Your toads will spy them and quickly come over to the bowl to feed.

Guppies

Feeder guppies are a staple food of many larger tropical fish. They also make a good food for your fire-bellied toads. If you balk at the idea of feeding live fish to your pets, you certainly don't have to do this. However, guppies do make a fine addition to the diet.

Guppies are sold at most pet stores that deal in tropical fish and are normally sold for a few cents each, or a small quantity for a dollar. Buy as many as your toads will eat in a day or two.

You can feed out the guppies by putting them right into the water section of your toad tank, by putting them in a shallow bowl, or by hand-feeding them. If your toads fail to catch any guppies for more than a couple days, net them out and put them in a small bowl; don't let the poor creatures starve to death in the toad tank. Of course, if you have live black, blood, or tubifex worms on hand, you could feed these to the guppies—at least until the toads get them.

Shrimp

Sometimes small shrimps are available at pet stores that sell tropical fish. Most often, these are live brine shrimps, but sometimes the freshwater gammarus shrimps are available. Fire-bellies eagerly accept these little crustaceans; they are probably similar to their natural prey.

These crustaceans, like the bloodworms, are high in pigments that will keep your toads looking great. You can let them go in the water section, but they might hide from your toads. It is probably best to feed them in a shallow bowl of water.

Brine shrimp are a saltwater species. If you buy them to feed to your toads, dispose of the water they come in, since the salt in the water could harm your toads. Usually the shrimp are packaged in plastic bags or small cups. Dump the whole contents of the container into a fish net. The water will pass through, leaving the shrimp behind; you can now dump the netted shrimp into your toads' aquatic area or feeding bowl.

How Often and How Much

Many pet stores recommend feeding fire-bellies and other herps only once per week. While most herps have an efficient metabolism and can go for long periods without food, small insectivores—like fire-bellied toads—have evolved to eat more frequently than that.

Bloodworms are one of several varieties of live fish food that your toads may enjoy.

How to Feed Different Prey

Prey	How to feed
Crickets and other insects	let loose in cage
Mealworms, wax worms, silkworms	in shallow bowl or feed by hand
Small earthworms	drop in front of toad or feed by hand
Aquatic worms	in shallow bowl with some water
Guppies	let loose in water section
Shrimp	let loose in water section or in shallow bowl with some water

Fire-bellies in the wild probably eat almost daily, and if there is a local abundance of a certain insect or crustacean, they will gorge themselves.

It is best to feed your toads daily or every other day. They can certainly get by if you go away for a weekend or short (three or four day) vacation. Remember that fire-bellies are active during the day, so feed them during the daylight hours. If you work, this probably means in the morning, just after turning on the tank lights.

How much you feed your toads depends on what you are feeding them. When feeding crickets, mealworms, or other sizable insects, each toad should eat approximately two or three insects. Make sure each toad in your group gets at least that many. Fire-bellies tend to gorge themselves until they are visibly swollen. Because fire-bellies are active toads, they rarely become obese.

When feeding other types of food, the amount to feed is a little tougher to gauge. About a thumbnail's portion of tubifex, bloodworms, or black worms should be enough for a fire-bellied toad. If you are feeding guppies, each toad should be allowed one or two.

More important than the numbers and amounts suggested here is how your toads respond to the amount you are feeding. Observe them daily. Do they seem to be losing weight? Feed them more often. Gaining weight? Skip a feeding weekly and see if that helps. Are their colors dull or faded? Try feeding your crickets more carrots and sweet potatoes.

Supplements

It used to be standard to recommend adding vitamin and mineral supplements to the diet of all herps. Because so little is known about the nutritional requirements of most reptiles and amphibians, and because too much of a vitamin or mineral is as dangerous as too little, the use of supplements has become more controversial. Some keepers maintain that if your feeder insects are properly gut-loaded, you never need to supplement. Others say supplement twice a week, once a week, once a month, or what have you.

It is probably best to supplement occasionally, but be mindful that you do not overdo it. If you are gut-loading the crickets and

A nicely plump yellow-bellied toad. Monitor the appearance of your toads to see if you are feeding too much or too little.

mealworms and providing diversity in the diet, you probably don't need to supplement the diet of your toads more than twice a month. If you are breeding fire-bellies, it is a good idea to increase the supplementation to once-weekly during the breeding season. The same goes for the toadlets.

Not all supplements are created equal. To get the best vitamin and mineral supplements for your toads, there are a few things to look for. First, only use a supplement formulated for herps, not one for birds, cats, or any other animals. Second, use a powdered supplement. Third, it is best to use separate vitamin and mineral supplements, because the minerals will cause some vitamins to degrade. Lastly, use a vitamin supplement that contains most or all of the vitamin A in the form of beta carotene. This helps prevent oversupplementation of vitamin A.

To add the supplements to the diet, put some of the powder in a jar or plastic bag. Add the day's ration of insects. Gently shake the jar; the powder will cover the crickets (you'll find that the supplements stick better to some insects, like crickets, than to others, like mealworms). Pick out the insects and feed them to your toads. Don't dump the contents into the toad terrarium, as that will cause unsightly and possibly harmful clods of soggy supplement to form.

Breeding Your Fire-Bellied Toads

Once you have been keeping fire-bellies for some time, you may decide that breeding them would be fun or educational or challenging, or a combination of all three. It is a trend in the modern herp hobby to breed our charges. This was not always the case. Only 20 years ago, it was enough of a challenge simply to keep most herps alive in captivity, let alone breed them. The hobby has come a long way in those two decades, and now it seems that most hobbyists are at least considering breeding their animals.

Before you commit to breeding your toads, ask yourself several questions and answer them honestly. If, after answering these questions, you decide that breeding fire-bellies is not for you, do not feel like you've failed or that you are somehow not as good of a hobbyist as others. Breeding isn't for everyone, and it does consume significant time, space, and money.

The first thing you have to ask yourself is what you will do with the baby toads (toadlets). Fire-bellied toads can produce numerous young. With only a small group of fire-bellies, you may find yourself up to your neck in tadpoles and toadlets. Because fire-bellies are common and cheap, they are not in high demand among herpers. Most pet stores can get them cheaply from their wholesalers, so they won't be willing to pay you very much for yours, even though yours will be healthy, captive-bred individuals. If you cannot sell or give them all away, you must be willing to keep them yourself. Don't even think of turning them loose! It is unlikely that captive-bred fire-bellied toads will be able to adapt to your local environment, so setting them free is likely to be a death sentence. The other possibility is that the fire-bellies will adapt to your environs. The presence of a new species of toad could wreak havoc on the local ecosystem. Many species of frogs and toads are in decline; the last thing they need is introduced competition.

Toads Gone Wild

In the 1950s, Australia imported great numbers of marine toads, *Bufo marinus*, to help control sugar cane pests (and earning the toads the colloquial name cane toads). Not only did the toads not eat the pests they were brought in to control, but in the absence of local predators, adapted and bred in explosive numbers. Today, the toads have spread and are out-competing many local frogs. Because of their toxicity, the toads are also endangering animals that attempt to eat them, including birds, snakes, and marsupials.

This is one of the best examples of why you should never release non-native species to your area.

Nuptial Pads

In most frogs, including fire-bellies, the males have bumpy mounds on the inside of their thumbs. These mounds, called nuptial pads, help the male hold onto the female during mating. In some species, these pads are large and are a darker color than the surrounding skin; however, in fire-bellies, they are not easily visible.

The next thing to think about is how able you will be to find tiny food for the toadlets and how willing you will be to perform all the increased chores—cleaning, feeding, watering, etc. If you suddenly go from a toad population of five to one of 50, you will have to spend a lot more time on these activities. You will also have to devote space to all these toads. Your feeding bills will increase, and depending on the lighting, heating, and filtration, your electric bill may go up as well.

Lastly, ask yourself why you want to breed fire-bellied toads. If you want to breed them to make money, remember how inexpensive

Fire-bellied toads often mate while floating on the surface of the water or resting on submerged plants.

Different Calls for Different Frogs

The calls of male frogs attract the females to mate. Each species of frog has a unique call that the female can readily identify. The calls are very specific. In fact, there are species of frogs that look identical to the human eye but have different calls. The females of each species never mate with the other species. This was shown to be true through genetic analysis. This research led to the realization that the common gray tree frog of North America was actually two species with different calls and gene pools but with an externally identical appearance.

and common they are. If you wish to breed them because you really enjoy the toads and want to learn more about them and how to raise these fascinating amphibians, then you will probably be a great fire-bellied parent.

Boys and Girls

If you are going to breed your toads, it is of course necessary to have at least one male and one female (more of each is helpful; read on). Therefore, it is helpful if you can tell the difference. Unfortunately, to the human eye, male and female fire-bellies aren't all that different. Adult females tend to look plumper and rounded, while males are more slender. The forearms of the males may be more muscular than the female.

It is usually easiest to sex fire-bellied toads by behavior. The males are the sex that calls, a soft "tink" noise. Additionally, the males will grasp passing frogs in hopes of mating with them. If they accidentally grasp a male, the molested male will struggle free.

Fire-bellied toads tend to breed best when kept in small groups. The recommendations vary as to how many of each sex is an ideal ratio. You should have at least two males, as the competition between them may help stimulate breeding. You will also want to have at least two females. If the size of your group permits, you should have more males than females.

Seasonal Breeders

Many species of animals are seasonal breeders. This means that they only breed at certain times of the year. Generally, the adults time their breeding so that the young will be born or hatching at a time of year when food is plentiful and the babies will have the best chance of survival. Amphibians who go through an aquatic stage may have the additional concern that the young must be ready to leave the water before the vernal pools dry up. Fire-bellied toads do not have this problem because they usually live in more permanent bodies of water.

In order to produce young at the appropriate part of the year, animals must notice clues in the environment. For most temperate species, these clues are the changes in the hours of daylight and the changes in temperature. Many temperate animals—fire-bellied toads included—go through a mild to complete hibernation, and it is this process of going into and coming out of hibernation that tells their bodies that it is time to breed. Of course, it is much more complicated than that, but if you remember that environmental cues determine when animals breed, you'll understand what you need to know to get your toads to breed.

This male is exhibiting the unken-reflex while still clasped to the female.

Fire-bellied toads do not enter a full hibernation, as their habitat only rarely freezes (the southern parts of the range never freeze). In nature, they become less active during the colder months of the year. Some of the other species of fire-bellies do come from areas that freeze, and these species go into complete hibernation.

To encourage your toads to breed, you have to trick them into thinking that the seasons are changing. You will be giving them an artificial winter, or cooling period, followed by an artificial spring. If all goes well, they will breed in your mock spring just as wild fire-bellies will breed during the real spring.

To simulate winter, you will have to keep your fire-bellies colder. If you are using any type of heater—a lamp, an aquatic heater, a heating pad—shut it off. Allow the cage to drop to room temperature. If your room temperature is too warm, you can put the cage on the floor of the house, where the temperatures should be substantially cooler than higher up on a shelf or tank stand. For the winter, the temperatures in the terrarium should be in the low 60s. Remember that fire-bellies do not tolerate temperatures below 50°F.

It will help promote breeding if you drop the water level in the aquatic portion of your toads' tank during the cooling period. Drop the water to about an inch deep or less. Some keepers eliminate the standing water completely during the winter and just keep the substrate moist.

A Cool Concern

If you are keeping live plants or other species of animals with your fire-bellied toads, make sure that they will not be harmed by the cooling period. If so, move the fire-bellies to another container for their simulated winter.

No Interlopers

It is best if you do not have other species of animals in the cage with your fire-bellies when you are attempting to breed them. The other animals may disrupt the mating or eat the eggs.

As you might expect, during the winter cool down, your toads will be sluggish. They will also have a reduced appetite. Cut back on the amount you are feeding the toads to avoid wasting food or having insects overrun the terrarium. Your toads will lose a little weight during the winter; do not be concerned unless one gets really skinny. If that happens, return that individual to normal keeping conditions as soon as possible and feed him heavily. Because they do lose some weight and because the winter conditions are hard on their little bodies, only put plump, healthy toads through the cooling period. Cooling and breeding underweight or unhealthy individuals will likely result in their deaths.

After about nine weeks, you can bring your toads back to normal temperatures and raise the water level. They will resume normal activity and appetite in a day or so. The females may come out of the cool-down looking especially plump and rounded, or they might grow rotund soon afterward. This rounded appearance is caused by the many eggs developing in the female's body. Start feeding your toads heavily, and remember to supplement the food with vitamins and minerals a little more frequently than normal. See the feeding

Another Cool Concern

Remember that you should only cool down and breed fire-bellied toads who are healthy and in good weight. Fire-bellied toads who are not in prime condition may not survive the cool down.

chapter for more information about supplements. Watch your toads when you feed them at this time. They may not be eating much, as they might be much more interested in mating than feeding.

Courting and Mating

Soon after the water levels return to normal, the males will start calling. Male fire-bellies call while floating in the water. The calling attracts the egg-laden females, and the males will grasp them about the waist with their forelimbs. The mating of frogs is called amplexus, and because the male fire-bellied toad holds onto the female around the waist, this type of amplexus is called *lumbar amplexus*. As mentioned, male fire-bellies are eager breeders, and they may initiate amplexus with other males, unreceptive females, aquatic plants, crickets, and other inappropriate things.

During amplexus, which may last as long as eight hours, the female will deposit her eggs while the male fertilizes them. If you have a sizable colony of fire-bellies, it is likely that more than one male will amplex with one female. In such cases, the eggs may be fertilized by more than one of the males. The female lays the eggs singly and in small clumps in the aquatic vegetation near the surface. Accounts vary as to how many eggs a female fire-belly can lay, but she certainly can produce at least 50 and perhaps as many as 300.

It is likely that your toads will spawn several times during the breeding season. Each time they do, the clutches contain fewer eggs.

Plants Will Help

Fire-bellies prefer to breed in open water that has a rich growth of aquatic plants. Having live plants in the water will help ensure breeding success. Along with the abundance of plants, make sure there are open areas for the males to float in and call from.

Male fire-bellies often mob one female. The eggs in one clutch may be fertilized by different males.

In between spawnings, feed the adults—especially the females—very well. Egg-laying is taxing on the female's body, so having enough nutritious food is important. Insufficient food will rapidly result in the decline of the female's health.

Once your toads lay eggs, separate the adults from them. The movements and activities of the adults may damage the delicate eggs. Also, the adults view any small moving objects as food, and this will include tadpoles and toadlets. It is probably easiest and less damaging to the eggs to move the adults to a new setup. However, when the eggs hatch and the tadpoles metamorphose into tiny toads, they may have trouble finding their food in the large and decorated terrarium that the adults inhabit. I find it better to move the eggs, realizing that this will cause some loss. It also saves the space and expense of having two terraria setups for the fire-bellies. A third option is to move the adults to a separate, small tank that is set up just for breeding. Then once the eggs are laid, you can move the adults back to their normal tank and care for the eggs and young in this more simplistic setup.

Amplexus in fire-bellies is called lumbar or inguinal amplexus because the male holds onto the female's waist rather than her upper back.

Caring for Eggs and Tadpoles

The water conditions needed to successfully hatch the eggs and rear the tadpoles are similar to those needed for the adults. The water should be kept very clean, but be careful not to disturb the eggs or siphon up tadpoles when cleaning the tank. The use of an air pump to

The embryos are just visible in these three-day-old fire-bellied toad eggs. The eggs hatch in four to eight days.

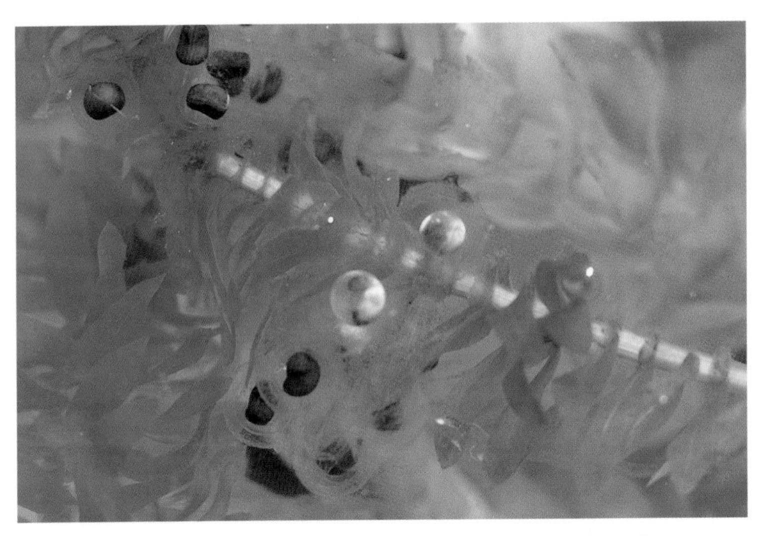

Eggs of the giant fire-bellied toad. All the fire-bellies prefer to lay their eggs in clumps of aquatic vegetation.

oxygenate the water is highly recommended. The temperatures used for the adults are adequate for the eggs and tadpoles. Development will be somewhat more rapid if the water is kept slightly warmer than normal. The ideal temperature is around 76°F. At this temperature, the tadpoles will hatch from the eggs in about four days. At lower temperatures, it may take as long as a week for the eggs to hatch.

When the tadpoles hatch, they will be tiny and dark brown to black in color. The tadpoles will spend their first few days motionless, stuck to the plants and sides of the aquarium. During this time, they are feeding off the remaining egg yolk in their bodies. After this period, they will begin to swim around and look for food.

The tadpoles are voracious and should be fed plenty of varied foods to ensure proper growth and development. They will eat tropical fish flakes and pellets, chopped earthworms, lightly steamed leafy green vegetables, and various freeze-dried worms and shrimps normally used to feed tropical fish. Remove uneaten food daily, and do partial water changes (remove and replace about half the water) two or three times per week.

Tadpoles Have Gills

If you look closely at the tadpoles, you may notice a projection in the stomach area. This is called the spiracle. It is actually the opening to the tadpole's gills.

When fed a generous and nutritious diet, the tadpoles will have visible hind limbs in about three weeks. They will have front limbs and start leaving the water in four to eight weeks, depending on diet and temperature. They will still have remnants of their tails, but these will be absorbed within a few days.

It is critical at this time that you have a way for the toadlets to leave the water and climb onto land, or they will drown. Emergent plants or driftwood leading from water to land works well for this purpose. If you have a sloping divider that separates the aquatic and terrestrial sections of the terrarium (see housing chapter), the toadlets should be able to clamber up that onto land. However you decide to construct the terrarium, observe your babies to be sure they can make it onto land.

Care of the Toadlets

It is at this stage of their development that fire-bellied toads are the most difficult to care for. Don't be discouraged if several die; that is fairly typical, especially for a novice breeder. Most fire-bellied toad breeders recommend keeping the toadlets in a simplistic or bare bones setup. This will better enable them to find food and make it easier for you to observe them. A simple rearing terrarium can be made from a clear container (such as a small fish tank or plastic critter cage) and a substrate of damp paper towels. You can, of course, opt for more elaborate housing, keeping the toadlets like you would the adults, but you are likely to suffer more losses. The temperatures used for the adults will be fine for the babies.

Although you might think that the small toadlets could never get out of the terrarium, think again. Their small size enables them to stick to the sides of the terrarium when wet and shimmy up the glass. Having some type of tight-fitting lid is important. If you use a screen top, be sure the mesh size is the smallest available. Otherwise, a few of your toadlets may escape.

Newly metamorphosed toadlets are tiny animals. Their size mandates that they be fed tiny food. Some items they can be fed are fruit flies, pinhead crickets (newly hatched crickets that are usually available by special ordering through pet stores or online suppliers), bloodworms, aphids, white worms, and hatchling silkworms. For optimal growth, the toadlets should be fed twice a day. Remember to remove any uneaten food items daily. Supplement the prey items with vitamins and minerals once a week.

Remember that fire-bellied toads don't develop their beautiful colors on their own. They require pigments from their diet. If you don't feed your toadlets prey containing the proper pigments now,

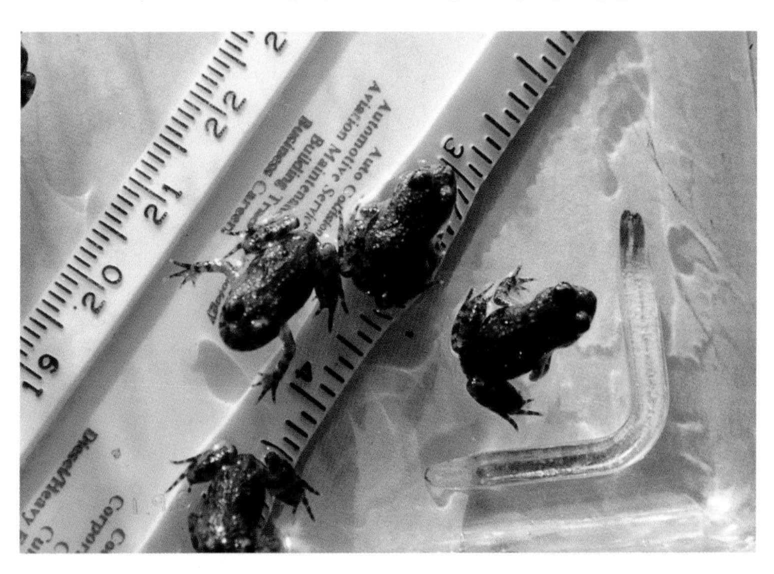

Fire-bellied toadlets are tiny. At three weeks old, each one is little more than a centimeter long.

they may never develop the bright belly colors that give them their name. Instead of a nice red or orange belly, your toads will be a washed-out cream or pale yellow. Bloodworms and gammarus shrimp will provide the color to your toadlets. Refer to the feeding chapter for more details.

Three-week-old toadlets climbing up the terrarium glass. They are just starting to show the bright belly color.

The toadlets will gradually start showing their brilliant adult colors. The toes and limbs seem to get colorful first, and the color spreads to the belly and throat.

If the toadlets are well fed, they will grow rapidly. Fire-bellied toads can mature in as little as eight months, but it is more normal for them to reach maturity in 12 to 14 months. Once the babies are near the same size as your original adults, you can put them in the same terrarium.

Unlike many other species of reptiles and amphibians that are bred by hobbyists, there are no established color varieties of fire-bellied toads. It is certainly possible that you could be the first breeder to produce a unique color morph.

Resources

MAGAZINES

Reptiles Magazine
P.O. Box 6050
Mission Viejo, CA 92690
www.animalnetwork.com/reptiles

Contemporary Herpetology
Southeastern Louisiana University
www.nhm.ac.uk/hosted_sites/ch

Herp Digest
www.herpdigest.org

ORGANIZATIONS

American Society of Ichthyologists and Herpetologists
Robert Karl Johnson, Secretary
Grice Marine Laboratory
University of Charleston
205 Fort Johnson Road
Charleston, SC 29412
www.asih.org

Society for the Study of Amphibians and Reptiles (SSAR)
Marion Preest, Secretary
The Claremont Colleges
925 N. Mills Ave.
Claremont, CA 91711
Phone: 909-607-8014
E-mail: mpreest@jsd.claremont.edu
www.ssarherps.org

Amphibian, Reptile & Insect Association
Liz Price
23 Windmill Rd
Irthlingsborough
Wellingborough NN9 5RJ
England
www.reptileallsorts.com/clubass.htm

List of Local Societies
www.kingsnake.com/society.html

WEB RESOURCES

Chinese Fire-Bellied Toad
www.anapsid.org/bombina.html
The Fire-Bellied Toad FAQ
www.amphibian.co.uk/bombina.html

Living Under World
www.livingunderworld.org

Kingsnake
www.kingsnake.com

Kingsnake Europe
www.kingsnake.co.uk

HerpNetwork
www.herpnetwork.com

VETERINARY RESOURCES

Association of Reptile and Amphibian Veterinarians
P.O. Box 605
Chester Heights, PA 19017
Phone: 610-358-9530
Fax: 610-892-4813
E-mail: ARAVETS@aol.com

RESCUE AND ADOPTION SERVICES

ASPCA
424 East 92nd Street
New York, NY 10128-6801
Phone: (212) 876-7700
E-mail: information@aspca.org
www.aspca.org

RSPCA
Wilberforce Way
Southwater
Horsham, West Sussex RH13 9RS
Telephone: 0870 3335 999
www.rspca.org.uk

Index

Measurement Conversion Chart

UNITS USED IN THIS BOOK
1 gallon = 3.7854 liters
1 inch = 2.54 centimeters
32°F = 0°C (water freezes)
75°F = 23.9°C

CONVERTING FAHRENHEIT TO CELSIUS
Subtract 32 from the Fahrenheit temperature.
Divide the answer by 9.
Multiply that answer by 5.